# IMAGINATION
## Key to Human Potential

A report of a conference sponsored jointly
by Pacific Oaks College, Pasadena, California
and The National Association for the Education of Young Children, Washington, D.C.

Polly McVickar, assisted by Mary Alice
Mallum, Grace Smith and other members of
the Pacific Oaks faculty.

All illustrations included in this book are enlarged
details from leaf, string, cardboard, and other
prints made at the "Imagination" conference.

Designed by Stansbury: Design Inc.

# CONTENTS

116498

# Foreword

Over the past three years, a new design of meetings has been initiated by the National Association for the Education of Young Children. In addition to scheduled national meetings, there is a plan for small regional conferences, organized in different areas of the United States for in-depth study of current trends and developments in educational thought.

The concept is perceptive and vigorous. Recognizing the work of the large meetings as significant in breadth of view and relationship to national concerns, it suggests that small meetings carry another value, that of depth and involvement not possible in national meetings.

These small groups serve not so much as "grass-roots" meetings, but rather as sturdy taproots, providing opportunity to "dig in," to question, discuss, try out ideas, explore new directions.

Here every participant can be heard, every idea valued and considered, and there is time for all aspects and implications. A sense of the whole educational view emerges because the parts can be fully known and experienced.

There are other values too. Out of a meeting centered in one geographical area comes impetus toward exploration of common concerns and a base for long range interchange among educators.

This meeting, IMAGINATION—KEY TO HUMAN POTENTIAL, took place in Pasadena, California, where participants came from nine western states, including Hawaii and Alaska. It was arranged through the resources of NAEYC and developed by the faculty and staff of Pacific Oaks College. Coordinated by Mrs. Polly McVickar of the College faculty, it drew on a committee of professional people engaged in early childhood education in the area .

The meeting began out of increasing concern that the processes of imagination are getting lost in a world that seems to value most what is predictable, safe, and neatly conforming. This group centered on the universal capacity to imagine, to find new ways and new ideas, and to ask the question, "what if." The purpose of the meeting was to experience, and out of that to find new ways to encourage and support the thrust of imagination in young children.

Thought and discussion grew around four areas of imaginative process.

**Imagination as the nucleus from which the individual moves out in all directions.**

**Imagination as a means of freeing the individual to try out experiences, feelings, ideas that go beyond conformity.**

**Imagination as the root of cognitive activity through discovery, exploration, knowing.**

**Imagination as it is enhanced or stifled by attitudes in the educational environment.**

**From . . . . . .**

**IN THE DREAMING WORLD OF CHILDREN**
**Dr. Robert Bainbridge**
**University of California**
**Santa Cruz**

**We forget how it is to be a child, and when we experience with children, we begin to regain a sense of that early time.**

**Children take in the whole world, and feel that they belong to every part of it.**

**They see it freshly with their muscles and their senses. How it looks, how it sounds, how it smells.**

**They utterly enjoy each moment, each thing as it is. They do spontaneously what Krishnamurti tells us, "see everything as it is."**

**Why not? What if? What else? These are the most logical, joyous questions there can be, as mind and imagination leap to encompass the wholeness of the world with the wholeness of themselves.**

# The Beginning

**"to exercise the muscles of the imagination"**
**—Phyllis Fenner, author**

The title of this meeting, IMAGINATION—KEY TO HUMAN POTENTIAL, is both a statement of recognition and expression of belief.

Sixty participants came as teachers of teachers, but more importantly, they came as human beings who already recognized the central, inherent capacity of all people to imagine. They came with recognition of the endless variety of human capacity, aware of the unpredictable readiness of every individual to ask new and perhaps preposterous questions of himself, to wonder, to find surprising associations, to trust hunches and intuitions, and to embark on new directions; with recognition that there is a human drive to try new ways, and make changes, with sureness of belief, but without certainty where a new idea will lead, or *if* it will lead anywhere. The drive is that strong, that persistent.

More than recognition was the underlying belief that however it comes about, imagination is the central capacity of a human being to draw together the wholeness of self. Starting with the persistent recurrence of the question, "what if . . .?" there comes the human determination to find out. From sensory feelings, sensory remembrance, thought, logic, humor, associations, a new concept, a new relationship grows; or a painting, a poem, a piece of music, a dance, a new view in science or a dream of something that has never been. Not to create a "masterpiece," but simply and humanly to extend the rich experience of living and find new knowledge of a self.

Here each individual could rediscover this human center, making his own choices, taking his own directions, selecting materials and tools, using time as the processes suggested. Not to be as children, but as mature individuals trusting their innate capacity to imagine.

The resources for this meeting were most importantly *ourselves.* Each of sixty teachers with a unique and individual capacity for imagining, would rediscover, and explore the languages of imagination.

Resources were also the writings and thought of those who are deeply committed to the processes of imagination . . . artists and scientists; musicians, poets, writers, dramatists; philosophers and theologians; teachers and students; fathers and mothers and children. In every way of life, the universal processes of imagination lead to new ways, new directions, new questions.

In the environment of this meeting, a setting equally valid for children or adults, we could see that imagination has no limits. When time and space and materials and tools are available, in a climate of openness and ease, it is possible to experience the joy of discovery, the challenge of new questions, the satisfaction of learning new skills, new combinations of ideas; and to know that the human imagination speaks by giving form to ideas through the languages of sound and rhythm, shape and color, words and meanings and feelings.

It was not a meeting for taking notes or listening to the words and theories of others. It was a time of experiencing the inner growth of imagination, stirring up the processes, finding new languages and reaffirming the total self. Not going away with an armload of mimeographed lists prepared by someone else; but carrying some new dimensions and new feelings and out of that, new understandings.

One member wrote,
**I know now that when I extend imagination in *one* direction, I stimulate the processes in myself and am open to the ways of imagination in *all* directions.**

# Imagination—The Ingredients

**"commitment to audacity"**
**John Burton, glass blower**

The ingredients of the imaginative process have been variously described by those involved in the arts and sciences.

Curiously, the basic elements are similar in every imaginative development, whether as direct as an experiment in cooking, as involved as the work of a painting, or as complex as an experiment in molecular chemistry.

First an idea . . . perhaps a hunch or intuition; or an image appearing out of past experience and feelings; or a vision of something seemingly fantastic and utterly impossible of achievement. Most often the individual himself does not know how the imaginative idea starts, but it seems always to contain a peculiar quality of energy and vitality that is exciting and does not let go. It becomes a "commitment to audacity" for there is belief in the idea without certainty of how or where it will go.

Next, a period of gestation, the time of "playing around" with the idea, getting the feel of it, testing it in thought, trying out its possibilities in imagination, and selecting or rejecting the aspects that seem unrelated. It is a period of clarifying the beginning focus.

Then, the time of hard work, when mind and muscles bring experience and judgment and skills together. Learning, changing, modifying, the idea takes form and is filled out with detail as other images are combined to make the meaning full.

Completion is that moment when the form is exactly in accord with the idea as it is conceived and enlarged with human insight. It has individual meaning but it is also a universal statement.

Ben Shahn, in his *Biography of a Painting* traces the growth of one of his works, *Allegory*. Beginning with an image, the remembrance of a fire experienced in his youth, the image grew in symbolic meaning. Other thoughts and images related and the whole became unified. Through the skills of painting, out of his knowledge of color and shape and balance, the whole was given outer form. Only the artist knows when it is complete, when the central idea is fulfilled.

Paul Saltman, molecular scientist, describes a similar process of growth and work, pushing to achieve an idea. He calls it **"like surfing . . . with a sense of excitement . . . and freedom . . . when the days are coming with everything hitting and you're seeing new relationships and the experiments work and the next and the next."**

In welcoming the participants of this meeting, Mrs. Marianne Wolman of Pacific Oaks faculty referred to one of the most magnificent expressions of imagination the world has known . . . the landing on the moon.

This was imagination on a global scale, and it is a fascinating thought that these processes of imagination appear to be the same as in individual experience.

Here was a global "commitment to audacity." It took centuries of time in development, and the work of hundreds of individuals in all parts of the world who labored tirelessly toward completion. The miraculous thing is that the idea itself never let go, that pursuit toward completion was based in belief and determination but without certainty.

Imagination does not end. We are still asking, "what if?" Can man live on the moon? Can man live in space? Can we reach Mars?

# The Languages of Imagination

**"validation of identity"**
**from "The Creative Experience"**

Imagination begins out of the continuing storehouse of images every individual accumulates in
the course of human experience. Images received
through the senses as shape and color and sound
and taste and smell and texture become part of
the growing individual and are continually stored
in sensory memory. Images never exist singly for
we take in the wholeness of experience; and the
image of a sunset, for instance, is not solely visual,
but carries with it, to some degree, response of
many senses.

More than that, it carries also a "feeling" content
which for every individual is his own, perhaps an
image symbolic of the end of day, the brightness
before darkness, or association with events or
people. We respond, as the poet Archibald
MacLeish has said, not simply as **"seeing"** but we
**"see feelingly."**

The richness of this individual storehouse depends
on the extent to which we continually enlarge the
capacity to receive sensory images, the awareness we develop for attention to details of sensory
experience and the readiness with which we are
open to the wholeness of impressions, including
thought and feeling.

Rudolph Arnheim, in *Visual Thinking,* has written,
**"there is today widespread unemployment of the
senses in every field of academic study because
they are seen as perception alone. Yet most know,
and take for granted that perception includes
intelligence, selection, discernment, and making
concepts of abstraction out of sensory imagery,
our first and final source of wisdom."**

The capacity to imagine, then, depends on vividness of awareness and sensitivity, and readiness
to allow the self to become fully involved with the
process of "taking in." The extent to which we
receive and recognize the complexity of sensory
images is what makes the richness out of which
new relationships, comparisons, ideas can grow.
Said in another way, when sensory images are not
felt, then thought can operate only at a
surface level.

And so the languages of imagination speak in two
ways—*to* us and *for* us.

18

When we respond to the imagery and insight a poet has found, we respond out of sensory experience and feelings. The imagination of the poet has meaning for us because human imagery is universal. Victor Hugo wrote, **"when I speak to you of *myself,* I am also speaking of *yourself."***

The languages of imagination are a "validation of identity" because an individual speaks uniquely out of his own experience. Art, literature, science, music, dance, ritual, are languages of imagination and our "taking in" capacity means receiving the languages of imagination as they are used by others.

When e. e. cummings writes of a new moon as **"thinner than a watch spring,"** it is the individual way he sees it, the unique comparison he finds. We recognize and take pleasure in what he points out because it not only is a surprising and new comparison but it carries with it a new and surprising reference to time.

When Marc Chagall paints a circus performer seeming to fly through the clouds, he is using imagery of color and shape to point out the marvelous freedom of the acrobat who must feel *as if* flying through the clouds.

In the same way, a scientific theory speaks to our imagination. A theory is a metaphor, a configuration of knowns that says, "it seems, right now, *as if* this is true." Science is dealing with uncertainties and with each new pursuit, each new thrust of imagination, it points out relationships which have not been noticed before, and pushes what is known further, though it will never reach the end.

Dr. Bronowski, in *Identity of Man,* has written about the language of imagination and how the "taking in" process occurs: **"Man constantly invents ideas to express what seems to him to lie behind the appearance of nature and to hold them together. The invention of these ideas and their interplay . . . is imagination, the making of images inside our heads . . . science is as much a play of imagination as poetry is."**

He writes further, **"Literature uses imagination to explore the alternatives of human action without** ever actually deciding for one rather than another."

"The knowledge we get from a poem or a play or a book, in contrast to the knowledge we get from science, does not tell us how to act but how to be. A poem tells us how to be human by identifying ourselves with others, and finding their dilemmas in ourselves. What we learn from it is self-knowledge."

The languages of imagination do not *tell* us, but through imagery ask us to think and feel out of our own experience.

This is also what two French psychologists, Roger Fretigny and Andre Virel, have pointed out. In their work, based also in art and mythology and anthropology, *The Imagery of the Mind,* they regard imagination as central in human consciousness because it systematizes the materials of experience and also takes apart both materials and systems in order to create new configurations.

There is another dimension of the "taking in" process. It was clearly demonstrated at this meeting and it is present in every classroom where an open plan of learning centers is arranged. This is the "taking in" and exchange as individuals, at any age, are using the languages of imagination, exploring and extending ideas through shape and color, through tone and rhythm, with body movement, with words and the sound of language, with experiences of science, or inventing with wood and wire and machines.

A Pacific Oaks student wrote about her experience of working with clay, "I always learn from others in the group . . . how they explore, what they discover. I select or reject or make variations, and thus find my own way."

In essence, this is the great value of open education and the learning center approach, that imaginative ideas catch fire from one person to another and possibilities of experiencing are widely extended.

We have these routes, and the languages of imagination speak *for* us. Not to make masterpieces but

20

simply and importantly to enlarge life experience. First of all, to speak *to* ourselves.

Through paint or clay, or dance, or music, or words we make clear to ourselves what we have found in life experience. Not for anyone else. It is a kind of rephrasing of experience, and sometimes showing us something we have not been aware of, or clarifying some aspect that went unnoticed.

By taking it out of ourselves, as Miriam Lindstrom writes, **"where we can see it,"** we find self-knowledge.

Where does the imaginative drive come from? Call it a spark, a hunch, a flash of intuition, a persistent question; there is no way of pinning it down. Harold Rugg writes in *Imagination,* **"it appears that the imaginative flash is never brought about by sheer force of will."** And indeed it often seems that the imaginative process is defeated when it is consciously searched for. It seems, and most will agree, it is when the individual can be loose and open and accepting of experiences, that the imaginative direction happens.

In *The Creative Process,* Brewster Ghiselin has brought together the writing of many artists, musicians, philosophers who have described the processes of imagination, and there is a curious similarity for all. The beginning of an idea, a period of playing around and trying out, and a period of gestation. Long effort in skilled work, times of discouragement, trial and error until the idea has reached completion, wholly satisfying to the individual who is the final judge of when it is finished and is the only one who can know the point at which the inner idea and its outer form are completely in accord.

*The Creative Process* contains the words of those who are professional in disciplined thought and skilled craftsmanship, who speak the languages of imagination in the arts, in science, in human relations. Yet the processes they describe are familiar to us and the languages of imagination are common to us all.

In the film by Saul Bass, *Why Man Creates,* he asks, **"Why *does* man create?"** And the answer is

simply and deeply, because **"I am I."** This is the validation of identity.

The *materials* of imagination are the materials of ordinary living. Wood, stone, glass; clay and earth; paper, cloth, wire, string; paint or words or tones of music; rhythm sounds or body movements, body stillness; machines; or patterns of thought, or new ways of human interchange. The list is endless and is limited only by the extent of individual capacity to see possibilities.

The *forms* of imagination and the combination of these forms will have as much variety as there are individuals. One imaginative beginning may grow to include a drawing together of color and shape and sound and feeling texture and movement, all making the idea complete.

The factor of *time* has no meaning. An imaginative idea may take years, or it may come to completion in an hour. Sometimes it is a long hard struggle to bring forth the idea, at other times everything seems to fit. One thing is clear. Once an idea has begun to grow, it will not let go. You have to keep at it.

The capacity is, in truth, a kind of central life spark that draws together the wholeness of self with all its diversity of intelligence and humor and wonder and understanding. And it is the power of imagination that it reaches into past experiences, or into a future that does not yet exist. And also that it enlarges the present.

Remembrance of past places and feelings and ideas; wonder about what has not been, what might be; reaching a depth of knowledge through images of fantasy; and heightened awareness of sensory relationships and intuitive responses in everyday experiences.

Take a tree, for instance, any tree you have known. Bring it into awareness through the sensory remembrance you have. Feel the bark, (rough? smooth?) smell of the sap, color of the blossoms, texture of the leaves; its sound in the rain, in the wind.

Your relationship to it . . . did you climb it, sit

under it, hide in its branches? Did it seem a refuge, a steady presence, a source of surprise for its changes with each season?

The wholeness of its meaning in life experience returns as you draw out the sensory images, and you feel again how it felt then. The more you reach for sensory images, the more they come clear as one suggests another. Seen again in the perspective of the present, you perhaps recognize some parts of the whole that you were not aware of at the time.

Through the languages of imagination, you might make a song, or a poem, about that past time and by **"exercising the muscles of the imagination,"** you can speak with depth of the images and feelings. It is a conversation with yourself, by which you enrich the experiences of the present by recreating out of past feelings.

Imagine, for instance, a camp fire. The colors and motion and smell. The line of sparks moving along the wood, the sparks flying into the air. The sound of crackling wood. You have the languages of imagination in which to tell of it—dance the motion of the flames, paint the many changing colors, make a song about the crackling, or a poem about the quiet time when only coals remain, and the sense of friendship is very deep. It is part of yourself and you extend and illuminate self-knowledge by using the languages of imagination.

In another way, with imagination you can think into the future. You create a new idea, you ask a new question, you design a place or a thing that does not exist.

You make in imagination a new kind of city, you imagine a kind of bird that has never been known, of extraordinary shape and color, or you make in a story, characters and places of some unknown place. Dreams, wonderings, the play of ideas can go in any direction.

Or you "play around with" a preposterous idea, perhaps an invention. You say "what if . . ." and try out new relationships, new values.

Robert Kennedy said, **"I dream a better world and**

**ask why not?"** That is imagination growing out of dissatisfaction with the present, and that question is a step to action . . . "why not?"

In fantasy, imagination goes beyond the limits of outer reality as we know it, yet, as in the fairy tales, we deal with the highest values we know, the central reality of life experience. Harvey Cox, in *Feast of Fools,* has written, **"In fantasy, we are not *less* conscious, we are *more* so."** By thinking in images we create a new view of the world. William Pene du Bois in *The Twenty One Balloons* uses the imagery of this story to draw together all the questions and values underlying the relationships of community living.

Ray Bradbury has said, **"Our ability to fantasize is our ability to survive."** Perhaps it is that important.

For instance, what kind of house would make possible the most complete kind of living? Throw aside all the conventions and building codes and rules, and let the plan develop out of values for living. Windows? Doors? Furniture? Space? Make a language of architecture that is based in human values.

And the capacity to imagine enlarges and enriches the *present.* To the extent that our sensory receivers are alive, the present is vivid in meaning and suggestion. Curiosity and exploration always yield new details, new responses; even the familiar is always different.

Saul Bass, in his film, *The Searching Eye,* points out the capacity of imagination to **"look at one thing and see another."** Comparing, seeing likenesses and differences, and out of that finding new awareness.

Robert Frost, when asked for his definition of originality, replied, **"I say originality is feats of association."** When imagination is open and one image connects with another, there is enlarged perception and new thought. Experience, as Arnheim says it, **"interacts with ideas through imagery."** Imagery that is unique for every person.

Hold up a piece of driftwood and ask the question

"What does it remind you of? What images do you see?" Every response is different . . . a dog lying down, the letter L, a Chinese character, a worm, a snake, a coil of wire, and one who said, **"it is like a giant key to the wall of a castle."**

Ask children what the moon reminds them of and there is an almost unending flow of comparisons . . . like a ball, a balloon, a finger nail, a rocking chair, a round hoop, a silver plate, a quiet place, a fairy circle. Here is the ready imagination that speaks in poetry and music and science and dance and feelings. Not in one direction alone, but drawing the whole person together—images out of the past, into the future and around the present.

The languages we have are common for all. Tone and rhythm; color and shape; words and sound and meanings; movement of muscles and body. These are the ways children speak freshly and spontaneously, and these are the ways we speak.

# Design for Experiencing
## Time, Space, Materials, Tools

**A PLACE FOR IMAGINATION—how it began**
People came to
the proper Hotel Dining Room
a most unlikely place.
They whisked off the tablecloths
moved all the furniture
opened all the doors
And they brought stuff and
other things
and books
and boxes
and lumber
and paint
and drums
and sand
and hammers
and clay
and leaves
and feathers
and mice
and markers
and
a
dead
fish
And the whole place
came alive.

Grace Smith
Pacific Oaks Children's
School

The real work of this meeting, experiencing the routes of imagination, came about as each individual made his own beginning. Thinking, watching, doing. These were starting points, out of which an individual developed his own use of time and space, exploring materials and tools, drawing out his own directions from curiosity, interest, skills, ideas, feelings.

*Space* was an open oblong room; *time,* a block of three days relatively unbroken; *materials* and *tools* available for discovery and experiencing.

Basically, the environment was designed with a flexible learning center approach, similar in plan to the open classroom and workshop approach emerging in education today. The basic centers— art, music, language, science—served as defined areas where the materials and tools of each were grouped. The center of the whole room became the area of work, changing throughout the meeting. Special interest areas spontaneously developed as experiencing and learning grew.

The design of the environment made it possible for the processes of imagination to happen. The participants brought it alive, each through individual capacity for imagination. For each it was a different route: experiences from a base of familiarity, trying out new ways and new directions, letting ideas take outer shape.

**"Now I know how children feel."** These words kept coming as each individual worked, finding a renewed sense of his own imaginative center.

The whole room was alive with discovery and ideas, with making and doing, with watching and thinking. The sounds here were the sounds of pleasure in exploring and finding unexpected and surprising things. The sounds of talk and laughter as each person shared ideas and asked new questions of each other; the sounds of music, and dance; the repeating sounds of hammer and saw; the words from films and records and tapes. All happening at once—changing, growing, rearranging, taking new directions—a total environment of imagining and learning, a place of **"exercising the muscles of the imagination."**

*Do my own your own story*

30

There were two parts in this design. *One,* the climate and atmosphere of the whole, and *two,* the workability of the learning centers.

Both are interrelated. The underlying, open plan makes possible a climate of freedom and trust and respect, because it engenders these qualities in the relationships of the group. The basic philosophy of open experiences shows in the flexible use of time, in readily adaptable use of space, and in the care that is taken for good materials and good tools and their availability for use. The climate of good feeling that comes out of design will always contribute to the excitement of ideas, and when it is lacking will work against the spread of discovery and learning.

This meeting began with a fundamental belief in imagination that created an atmosphere of trust. Trust in the human processes of imagination, trust in the purpose of the meeting, trust in the arrangements and underlying plan. Fundamentally, it was founded in the trust of individuals with each other and it was as tangible as the materials and tools.

Because the plan was an open one, directions and experiences could evolve. They could not be predicted and were not determined ahead of time. The work of the group would grow and change as the individuals themselves. The meeting was itself **"a commitment to audacity."**

■ **Climate**

There were specific elements of the environment that seemed significant in the whole climate of feelings.

The meeting was arranged with a span of time not broken into segments. No one needed to watch the clock. No groups were separated off into time slots or into other areas. Many groupings of talk and discussion grew out of the work but they happened easily, spontaneously and were part of the whole.

Every individual was using *time* in his own way. The faculty of Pacific Oaks was ready to answer questions, or help with specific needs for additional materials or tools; but they were working also, trying out new ways and pursuing new ideas. No one was "telling" another because each was engaged in his own processes of imagination. *doing own thing*

The arrangement of *space* was important. The centers were defined only by low dividers which made the whole room open and gave the sense of freedom. Because the dividers were low, everything going on in the room could easily be seen and shared. One participant remarked, **"I felt that I belonged to the whole room."** *space*

The open plan also invited and made possible the interrelationship of all areas. An experience that began with art might well become also a total effort in which dance and music and science and languages were drawn together in a unification of the whole.

Arrangement of the centers also gave evidence of this *flexibility* and interrelationship. Many centers were stocked with the same materials. For instance, there were rocks and pebbles in every center—in art experiences they were used for making prints, or glued together to make rock sculpture; in the science area, they were explored with a hammer to **"find out what's inside;"** in the music area, a handful of pebbles rattled together in the hands became a kind of natural beat to a record or a dance; in the language area, someone wrote a poem about rocks.

The arrangement of the centers also meant awareness or organization and *stability.* In the sense that the materials and tools were always grouped together, they could easily be found when needed to extend ideas. **"Will it be right here tomorrow?"** was one of the questions that came, and was evidence of how involved the processes of imagination are. What is not finished one time, is carried over to the next day and the next, because an idea takes time. It is necessary to know that the materials are stable and will continue to be available. An imaginative idea keeps growing, apart from the actual making.

Climate has another aspect too—the vividness of the environment. Mobiles hanging and moving; bright cloth laid on a shelf; flowers and plants; photographs and prints on the wall. And always

32

work-in-progress, such as drawings and paintings still growing and changing, a scientific experiment being constructed, a wood structure not yet completed. These are the evidences of thinking and learning and making that heighten the climate of imagination.

Here are some words and thoughts about climate, as they came from the group:

**The importance of freedom**

**Every person was in charge of himself. There was no map, no set of directions that indicated where to go. Each person made his own exploration as ideas and interest grew.**

**There was freedom to fail and learn from that. Freedom to talk, make friends, watch and share ideas. Freedom to question, to suggest other centers, other arrangements in the room. It was a place we all belonged to and it grew and changed with the flow of ideas.**

**A relaxed atmosphere in which to experience, explore, relate in an informal way. Time to move at your own pace with no set time limits.**

**I am not the same person as when I went to this meeting, because of what I heard, saw and felt. Mrs. Molly Morgenroth gave the mood, a complete oneness in purpose of everyone. We were all working toward a common goal, imagination as freeing the individual. The learning centers made possible great satisfaction in creating and expressing ideas without interruption.**

**Molly Morgenroth's song, "I Wonder What Would Happen If," expressed this openness for me.**

**There was a freedom to look, to take your own route of doing or do nothing but watch.**

**Ideas caught fire. I could watch everything that was going on while working on my own.**

**I never have time to do these things for myself so it was a deep pleasure to be in a relaxed situation where things were set up for creativeness.**

**As a director, I have found little time for creative**

**things. This gave me a reservoir of good feeling that will last a long time.**

## A sense of trust

Trust in one's own capacity and in the innate capacity of every person to discover, to want to explore, try out; in the basic desire to **"make,"** to relate one thing with another, perhaps for a meaning, perhaps simply because **"I like it that way."** The idea that people trust each other, and there is no judging, no right or wrong in making, in imagining.

**What is good and deep and strong for the individual is good. No idea is too impossible to try.**

*Her feelings*

**A personal strengthening of self concept . . . I CAN . . . that will give genuine strength in my words "You Can" to students . . . for if I can, surely so can they.**

**Reinforcement of my own ideas and thoughts about the creative process of teachers and children, and awareness of the great need for all of us to break down the walls of outmoded values and open ourselves to new ways.**

*Read*

**Reinforcement of my own ideas . . . inspiration for what continues and the ability to return and convey it.**

**Joy . . . assurance in ideas, materials, literature . . . food for thinking many provocative thoughts. Beauty and substance in the words and slides of Dr. Robert Bainbridge.**

**The most meaningful group experience I ever had . . . much more than those with a specific topic for discussion. A joyful experience to create in an atmosphere of freedom and acceptance, with a small number of people.**

**The relationship with people was important, and the dance experience with Hilda Mullin gave particular insight to my concern for this area of expression.**

**It came at the right time, just as I was beginning to live more openly, and my approach has been**

34

affirmed and become more so since these three days.

I could see the meaning of these experiences for others, but I was not ready to move that way myself.

It is not clear to me how learning takes place in an environment such as this.

### Feeling of respect—for self and others

The room became alive with people moving, working, trying everything out, working very hard at one thing, putting that aside for the moment to work at something else. Talking and laughing, working and watching. Imagination is both private and group, sometimes alone, sometimes with others.

I had lost touch with the process of imagination and I had forgotten how necessary it is to oneself.

There was opportunity for all ways, for the rhythm of the processes, to stop and wonder, to work, to try something else, and when it was completed, a safe place for it to be kept and valued.

A reinforcement of my own instincts, my own ideas, questions, and my ability to put those into action.

You learn a great deal just by watching others. How good to move freely and talk with others engaged in the same pursuits.

It confirmed for me, once again, that I enjoy being free to discover "for myself." It is great to be with people who have the same concerns, goals, values. It recharges the batteries.

I had the opportunity to view myself apart from my immediate family, friends and daily environment, to look inward and become more aware of the inner me. There was time to meditate and follow up on my feelings with creative action . . . which I chose simply because it felt good to do so.

It takes time to learn to think of learning in a different way. I am beginning to understand how "doing" is learning.

Dr. Albert Hibbs gave me a whole new view of science . . . that it is not finished, not firm in its conclusions, but open ended, growing, changing all the time.

At first I felt guilty not to be taking notes and making lists to take back . . . and then I decided to enjoy the experiences and this freshened attitude was, in truth, the most valuable thing I would take back.

## ■ The Centers

Four basic centers were arranged around the room, from which other areas of interest spontaneously developed as experiences grew and developed.

These centers—art, music, science, language—remained as the base where materials and tools for each were grouped. We could say that these are the fundamental areas of learning that concern education, at all levels, and out of which discovery and exploration lead to endless variation of experience and direction.

Interestingly, we could also draw a parallel with the concerns of this meeting in experiencing the processes of imagination. Basic in education, these centers also defined the languages of imagination. These are the ways imaginative thought speaks *to* us, and they are also the directions the imaginative capacity of individuals uses to speak *for* us. In essence, education is itself speaking the languages of imagination.

Wilferd Peterson, in *The Art of Living,* writes, **"Without imagination, thought comes to a halt."** Out of exploring shapes and colors and form in art, we find new and unique ways to speak; out of tone and beat, rhythm and body movement, we speak through music and dance; out of words and rhyming and language sounds, we speak in poetry and prose; out of exploring how things grow, testing the natural laws of our world, discovering new knowledge, we speak in the sciences; and through endlessly exploring the relationships of human beings, we speak with feelings and ideas.

The centers make possible the experiences of trying out ideas through making and doing. It is learning and knowing through process, a kind of conversation of the individual with himself. As ideas and feelings pull you forward—in any of these directions—the imaginative idea begins to have outer form. You tell yourself through colors or tone or shape or sound what you have found and what you know. As it begins to take shape, you are aware of details you had not noticed before. The idea is heightened and enlarged.

The idea and the making come together, and the sense of completion will not happen until the outer form comes as close to the central idea as you can make it. The work of imagination goes on until the idea and its expression fit.

And because as human beings we are acquainted with and understanding of human dilemmas and experiences, others can respond to the idea in its outer form. Communication takes place because of human understandings and feelings.

## THE ART CENTER
**"Art is not an embellishment . . . it is a unique mode of discourse giving access . . . to self-knowledge."**
**Sir Herbert Read**

The first function of the center was to provide access to an array of materials and tools. It has been said that simply the selection of a color **"because I like it"** is in itself a creative act. You affirm yourself in that choice, and you continue affirmation with the selection of brushes or sponges, rough paper, shiny paper, or the size and shape of wood pieces. You select and reject in terms of the imaginative idea you want to give form to.

In art, the point of beginning is not in aiming for a product, but in knowing that as it goes, the idea will change and grow and out of that, use of tools and materials will also change.

Art is not copying anything. The artist Dubuffet has said this in describing his own work. **"It seems to me that to apply oneself to cataloguing faithfully the real measurement of things is a wholly valueless operation. What strikes me as**

37

interesting is to restore in representation of an object, the whole complex system of impressions that we receive in the normal situations of ordinary life, the manner in which it strikes your affectivity and the forms it assumes in our memory. . . ."

The variety of materials and tools was of first importance in this center, making opportunity for choices. Each material and each tool has specific qualities and properties, and each serves to express an idea in a different way. The idea determines the selection.

*material*

Many experiences with color. Paint in a variety of shades and texture, some thick, some thin. Opportunity for mixing to make a combination of colors. Colored pencils, charcoal, marking pens and colored inks, all with different qualities.

*paint*

A variety of tools. Especially a range of brushes in many different sizes—wide, narrow; soft or stiff. Each one expresses a different feeling. Or sponges, strips of felt, pieces of wood or cork, spools, wire mesh . . . all of them tools that make an imaginative idea take form.

*tools*

Many kinds of material to work on—all sizes of paper, and a variety of shapes, long and narrow, round, triangular. Many textures, shiny, rough, smooth; corrugated; IBM cards; boxes, cloth, tile, wood, graph paper, blueprint paper. The list can be endless. The more there are choices, the tools and materials themselves make suggestions for working.

Pods and grasses and leaves; wood and shells and rocks; feathers and straws; pipe cleaners and pot cleaners; toothbrushes and vegetable brushes. Everything is possible in the processes of imagination.

Supplies are important and serve in many ways; glue, scissors, wire, paper clips, rubber bands, thumb tacks, yarn and thread, string of all sizes. Everything in the art centers was used, often in surprising ways.

Two tables for work with *clay* became a separate center. Sacks of pottery clay were available,

enough for everyone to have a large piece.
Pliable, yet firm in texture, the terra-cotta color
gives a feeling of working with earth itself.

It takes time to get acquainted with clay. Try every
motion you want, it responds just as you do it.
Punch, poke, pull; smooth it, press into it; pile it
up, spread it out, make holes in it. The color and
the shadows change. Each form that appears
suggests and leads you on.

Stand up to slam it on the tables, press elbows or
knuckles into it. Or wrists or knees. Walk around
to see it on all sides. It holds the impression of
your bones and your muscles until you change it.

It can be a thing you know, a thing you remember,
a place you imagine that you invent, a fantastic
animal that has never been. Or it may be a feeling,
or a shape you like. It is your own self in the clay.

It is a very personal experience because you are
involved with it directly. Your hands are your tools.

From . . .

**PREPRIMARY ART—Parent and Child**
**Polly McVickar, Pacific Oaks Faculty**

The child who paints a house with wings may be
saying how he feels about his house. He may be
saying that the pleasant feeling of being in his
house is "as though" he were flying . . . and it is
also possible that in the process of painting it
simply seemed like a good idea to paint wings
because they looked good there. We have no
way of knowing and we should not try to.

*a child's painting.*

A child who makes a pencil drawing of people
running through the air may be using the most
graphic way he can think of to express speed.
People run on the ground, yes; but he is using an
image here to show *how* fast they are going, as
fast as though flying, as fast as birds.

And a child who paints a tree walking, is so at
home with the language of imagination, that he
can personify a tree, and it is "as if" a tree could
walk like a person, or bend down with branches
like arms.

This is the free roaming imagination of children
who constantly make what seem to us surprising
relationships but have all the logic of imagery. A
child free and unafraid to try new ways, is certainly not concerned to make a "copy" of what
he has experienced. Indeed it is nearly impossible for him to copy anything because he re-
members, and sees, and feels all at the same
time.

Publication of the National
Art Education Association

40

As each worked, comments and thoughts came:

**I should have clay around the house all the time.
Not just for children, but most of all for me.**

**I see why children work with it so long. It holds
you and it keeps suggesting other ways.**

**It feels good. It feels cool and has an earth smell.**

**As you work your thoughts go in many directions.
It seems to free your feelings and your
remembrance.**

**Just letting the shapes come seems important.
It doesn't have to be a *thing*.**

**I have pounded this so hard my shoulders are
tired. But I like that feeling.**

**You need to stand up to work with clay. Your
body is more free.**

Teachers
Comments

Another center developed—the tables of *wood
pieces,* all sizes and shapes. This too is experience with three dimensional shapes, but unlike the
work with clay, it is not as much in making forms
as in assembling and combining and adding
shapes.

wood

The wood was itself a sensory experience of smell
and touch and color. Pine wood, redwood;
shingles, slabs, scraps from a cabinet maker's
shop; branches from dry bushes, stiff grasses.
And pebbles and rocks. And sawdust.

The supplies here included glue and wire and
tape, in holding constructions together.

Manipulation is complex. It can be vertical or hori-
zontal, as you fit sizes together. Sometimes it
works, sometimes it requires change and modifi-
cation. You learn what is possible, what will balance, what will hold. You discover the beauty of
shadows and the different colors of wood. You
like the wavy lines of wood grain and your fingers
feel the small ridges. Your idea grows and
changes as the work progresses. There is no one
way. Your idea tells your hands, but the idea must
"hang loose" as you deal with the properties of

the wood itself. In a sense, you are dealing with architecture.

Another center, similar in a way, yet different, was the table of collage materials. Cloth, paper, cardboard, pieces of plastic, boxes. Everything could combine, either sewn together, or taped or wired. Mobiles grew with yarn and string and wire and leaves. Dry branches were decorated with colors and shapes of tissue paper, crepe paper, torn magazines. The form could be changed, or added to, or taken apart and given a new start with other colors and shapes.

Pebbles and rocks of all sizes were glued together and became rock sculpture, rough and interesting because the form grew into unexpected shapes.

The more you work with materials, the more you gain experience in making choices, in selecting and rejecting a material, in ease of trying out. You learn as you work. The result is not as important as the sense of experiencing and drawing out your capacity to imagine.

These are some of the words and thoughts:

**I never knew that white glue would hold rocks. I have two sculptures to take home.**

**Everything, but everything can be combined. The whole world is open if you let it be that way.**

**Things don't *have* to be one way, or the way they always have been. They can be what a person, a child, wants it to be.**

**It is good, if you like it. There is no right way and no wrong way.**

**It is your own private exploration that matters. It speaks for you.**

One center was arranged outdoors. This was the *woodworking* area where Bill Baker and Mel Suhd, with their staff from the Creative Environment Workshop, set up materials and tools and provided help in the variety of projects and inventions that began.

Materials were wood and Tri-Wall and plastic tubing. Tools included nails, saws, hammers, cutting tools, and power drills. The actual use of power tools was a new experience for many and was an introduction into a whole new experience. As designs and ideas grew, either in planning material for classrooms, or for making musical instruments, using muscles and know-how in managing the tools was a new dimension.

What Piaget has said of childhood is true in all learning, **"they must be able to try things out to see what happens, manipulate objects, pose questions . . . seek answers."** This is how the potential of human capacity unlocks.

**We made everything from musical instruments, to book racks, and other things.**

**I never knew I could run a power saw. I was scared at first, then I trusted the person who showed me how. And I did it. I did it myself. That was the great thing. Now I know I can, I will.**

## THE SCIENCE CENTER

**"From the beginning . . . a child should experience the joy of discovery."**
**Alfred North Whitehead**

This is the place where wonder and curiosity begin, curiosity about nature, about the world, about ourselves, about plants and animals and fish; and about space. Curiosity turns into action and it is the place to explore, investigate, and ask questions of yourself. Everything challenges you to know and find out for yourself. You find your kind of knowing.

*Sensory investigation:* The first line of learning is through the receivers we possess, the senses to hear and smell, taste and touch and see. These raise the first questions, the first directions and the beginning answers.

A piece of cheese covered with mold . . . how does it grow, how does it happen, where does it come from?

A rusty pipe, how did it get that way? Look at the layers and the colors underneath. What is rust? What makes that happen? What might keep if from happening?

Explore everything and find the words to tell yourself what you find. What is rough? What is smooth? What is heavy? What is hard? Define small differences in words like damp, moist, wet, soggy, sopping; tell yourself exactly what you find.

**From . . .**

**IMAGINATION IN SCIENCE**
**Dr. Albert Hibbs, Senior Scientist**
**Jet Propulsion Laboratory**
**Pasadena**

Science is not closed or ended. We are not dealing with certainties, we are working with uncertainties.

We move from what seems to be true in a given
arrangement of the known, but with each push
forward, it changes.

We build on the body of knowledge as it is
known, but what determines the push comes out
of being alert to new associations, new insights,
new possibilities that may lead somewhere. Or
may not.

For a child, it is more important that he know a
rock, for instance, by taking a hammer to pound
it and find out what is inside, how it looks, how it
feels, what forms are there.

Source books should come second, after the first-
hand sensory investigation and manipulation.

Words about the shape of things. What is round, or oval, or square, or oblong? What is a sphere? Cube? What is a cylinder? A torus? This is beginning geometry.

Find the likenesses, find the differences. What about the words transparent, translucent, opaque?

Find the differences. Heavier than what? Narrower than what? Shorter? Lighter? Faster?

After sensory knowing comes *manipulation*. Here in the center were materials for **"finding out."** Take a dandelion apart, or a sunflower. Find the petals, the pistil, the stamen. Where are the seeds? Take a small branch. Feel the bark, peel off the layers, whittle it to see the grain, cut it across to see the rings. Explore it and then find a book and illustrations that help in naming. Here is beginning botany. A book comes after your first exploration.

Take a rock, weigh it, see its colors, follow the lines with your finger. Take a hammer and find out what it's like inside. Collect all sizes and shapes and colors of rocks. Some are softer than others? Some chip easily, some are hard? Here is beginning geology.

Watch hamsters and rats. They breathe and move as we do. They need water, and food. Compare a small rat skeleton, to see the bones, the skull, the ribs. Cut open a fish to find gills and backbone.

There is beginning *physics* here. What moves requires energy, such as ourselves using a broom, moving or turning an egg beater; the energy from a motor to drive a car.

There is beginning *chemistry*. Cooking is the process where matter changes its form. Eggs become scrambled. Pudding thickens with heat, stays firm in cooking. Evaporation, steam, are all part of the process of change.

*Tools and materials:* Tools for knowing, like magnets, and scales and magnifying glasses. Jars and cans for exploring water; scales for weighing; yardsticks and rulers for measuring. Tongs for holding something while looking at all sides.

48

*Books and source materials:* Authors, Cooper, Branley, Podendorf, Selsam and many others; pictures and diagrams. Books of animals and birds, books about space and rockets.

A place for everyone to have a collecting box, for keeping the interesting and unusual things you find, a shell, a castoff bird's nest, a dead beetle. A notebook where you might paste pictures that make you wonder.

Dr. Albert Hibbs says of science it is never completed, there are no final answers. And so for each person, you find your own answers to your own questions, and more questions and more answers.

**I never thought of so many ways to investigate water.**

**Using a knife to cut across a plant stem is such an obvious and simple way to demonstrate how a plant grows.**

**I think caring for animals, or fish, is one of the most important learning experiences children have. Not only for physical care, a place to sleep, place to play and run, food and water, but also the awareness not to hurt as we do.**

**Asking yourself questions is the beginning of knowing everything.**

**Asking questions about things that seem small and unimportant always leads to a whole lot of other questions.**

## THE MUSIC CENTER

**"music is a language without a dictionary"**
**Aaron Copland, musician**
**"dance is truth itself."**
**Martha Graham, dancer**

First materials for *listening.* Shells to hold to the ear, pine branches to move back and forth, listening to the soft swish, gourds that rattle, bones for tapping, small pebbles to click in the hand with sound and rhythm. And grass held between the thumbs to blow through. And a cricket in his small cage . . . listen to the beat of a cricket song.

Then *instruments.* Many sizes of bells, cow bells, small Christmas bells, temple bells . . . all with different tone and different reverberation. A brass bowl when touched with a wooden stick makes music. Listen to the very last small reverberation as you count each one. Drums of every size, some from Africa and India, others made from boxes with varnished muslin stretched over. Explore them with your hands and fingers. Not with sticks but with yourself, so there is nothing between you and the sound. Make it fast or slow; heavy or light. Try the sides, try the edges to find the differences of tone.

Other instruments here also. A marimba, casta-nets, clappers; harmonicas and tambourines; rattles of every size. Guitar and autoharp. Chimes of shells.

Humming, singing, beating a rhythm, music is a language of your own feelings, always possible wherever you are.

Song books make starting points and give the pleasure of singing together, children and teachers. Malvina Reynolds', *Tweedles and Foodles for Young Noodles;* Ruth Seeger's, *American Folk Songs for Children;* Chroman's, *The Songs Children Sing,* a collection drawn from all over the world; and Molly Morgenroth's, *Story Songs That Spin Themselves,* containing guides for teachers that are exceptionally helpful in understanding children and music.

A record player for accompanying instruments, or just for listening. Records for singing with, such as those by Marcia Berman, Sam Hinton, Pete Seeger, Marais and Miranda. Records for hearing and knowing how different instruments sound, a clarinet, cello, trombone. Records for dance and movement, such as *Missa Luba, Dance Time in Scandinavia,* or the *Karmon Israeli Songs and Dances.*

As the meeting developed, instruments were made. Cocoanut shells became clappers; tubing was made into flutes, pieces of wood strung with squidding line became stringed instruments; a hollow piece of wood became a tone block, and slabs of wood strung together made a kind of marimba. Spontaneously a group gathered to accompany a record and from that a dance began that drew in the whole group.

Thoughts from the group:

**I found that adults can really meet with children in music.**

**I like the same things they do, listening and moving.**

**There is a great variety of music on records, not just children's records.**

**I discovered Marcia Berman here.**

**The music books were good resources, especially _The Songs Children Sing,_ edited by Eleanor Chroman.**

**Molly Morgenroth's songs made me know that music can be as natural as talking.**

**I have learned to listen to children as they sing and chant, sometimes joining with them.**

From . . .

## STORY SONGS THAT SPIN THEMSELVES
Molly A. Morgenroth

If young children are in an environment where
they trust and communicate with adults, they will
sing as naturally as they speak—"weaving"
chant and speech just as they manipulate other
materials—in the pursuit of finding out and
expressing feelings.

If there is one essential truth about the creative
use of music with children and with teachers, it
is that the music should grow from the life of the
persons involved. It can be an exploration of
great range and meaning if looked at in this way.

The creative bubbling-up of chant, song and
dance in daily life with young children means that
teachers and parents who are watching and
listening draw this into the mainstream of experience. The spontaneous "bubbling" brings unexpected color, design, imagination and meaning.

For the teacher, there is no substitute for a mind
well stocked with songs. You need to know songs
as you know stories and poetry, so they are
always ready.

An ordinary voice is all you need to start singing.
Your love of rhythm and melody will tend to
improve the voice you have.

Enjoy.

## DANCE, A MOTOR SOURCE OF IMAGINATION
Hilda Mullen

Dance is a language of gestures; gesture is the outward expression of a "felt-thought."

Gesture is the sign language of an emotion.

In dance we are concerned with—

> organism as-a-whole rather than split body
> and mind
> feeling rather than thinking
> body action rather than verbalization
> intuition rather than science
> a creative way of discovery and knowing.

A primal awareness was known to primitive man as he danced his fears and his joys. A child understands this too as he is a "neo-primitive." One child expressed his feeling about this:

> "I like creative dancing because it's where
> you're just playing; there isn't any special way
> to do anything. The things you do are special
> in your own mind. You can't keep it in there
> any longer, you just have to burst it out in
> some way—just dance it out."

Movement forms the matrix from which the child organizes and experiences himself, and the world around him. It develops a self-awareness that helps the child integrate his experience.

## THE LANGUAGE CENTER

**"Having ideas is the only freedom."**
                                                    **Robert Frost**

*Language*

Perhaps this is the basic premise of a language
center, ideas. The more you have to think about
and talk about, the more you become aware of
how to use language. Ideas drive you to use words
to tell and talk and ask and answer. Ideas at any
age, need words to say them.

This center began with ideas.

Many pictures to talk about. Not simple object
pictures, but photographs of action and feeling,
of people doing things. Rachel Carson's *Sense of
Wonder*, Reich's *Children and Their Fathers*,
Ylla's *Animals*.

A changing assortment of things to look at, feel,
taste, listen to. An old alarm clock, some bells, a
clay figure of a rabbit, a railroad spike, a moon
stone to see the light through. Things to discuss
and then find words to say what you have found.

Books of rhyming sounds, to hear aloud, to say
with the reader, to remember and say at other
times. From *The Puffin Book of Nursery Rhymes*,
by Iona and Peter Opie, *Nonsense* by Edward
Lear, *Rocket in My Pocket* by Carl Withers,
*Rimbles* by Katherine Evans, and *Tongue Tanglers*
by Charles Francis Potter.

Make the rhyming sounds, add some other
rhymes. See how the words feel as tongue and
teeth and cheeks make the sounds. Jump rope
rhymes, counting out rhymes, rhyming games, all
part of the process of "limbering up" the mecha-
nisms of speech. And the more you are good at
making sounds—reproducing the sounds of animals, or machinery, or saying rhymes—the more
you come to know that the sound your teeth and
tongue make, is the sound on the printed page.
And that is where reading begins.

Books are here, to look through and listen to.
Books with good words in them, words like "hori-
zon," "flabbergasted"; or a new way of saying
things, "even the wind has stopped breathing," in

Jack Tworkov's, *The Camel Who Took a Walk.* Or Beatrix Potter's *Squirrel Nutkin* who was "impertinent," or Kipling's *Just So Stories,* with its alliteration of "the great gray greasy Limpopo river," in *How the Elephant Got His Trunk.*

Books full of the sound of language, its rhyming and repetition and words.

From . . .

**I CAN'T THINK HOW TO SAY IT (manuscript)**

Grace Smith, Pacific Oaks Children's School

*About me:*

My nose is
Smelling popcorn.

When I swing
I close my eyes
And I feel higher.

Ice cream
Scares my teeth
It scares it
Cold.

I am a girl
I am a girl
Yes, I am a girl.

*About us:*

A sister is a friend
A brother is a friend
And me is a friend
Of you.

The teacher is
For when it's
Too hard.

*About the world:*

How old is a baby
When it's born?
It's zero old.

Clay is
Icky gluey gooey fooey
Stuck
Yuk.

When I jump
My shadow jumps
Because it's me.

It's raining
It's pouring
Slippy sloppy morning

I got a drink of water
Drink of water from the sky.

Fog is
Like rain

Look at
That leaf
Do a somersault.

But not
So much.

Nature things to explore and talk about. Take a geranium leaf. Feel it, smell it, taste it. "It's soft like cloth, it's like a scalloped doily, like a scarf, like my puppy's ear." Take a magnolia leaf. One side is like suede, its veins are like bones, it is like a feather, like a hand, like a fish. It curls like a hand, it looks like a boat.

This is where imagination begins. You look at one thing and see another. One thing reminds you of another. Poetry starts, telling stories begins, "writing" starts when the teacher is there to write down a story, until later when the children write themselves.

Some of the tools for knowing language and words: alphabet books, letter shapes, a typewriter, a printing set; notebooks, pens, pencils, marking pens, crayons; magazines with pictures and letters; scissors, glue, paper; a tape recorder, a record player, a listening center with earphones.

And always time for talking because the more you put ideas into words, the more both the ideas and the language grow.

Comments about language experiences:

**I never realized how important the nursery rhymes are. I never really listened to them.**

**When you hear them just for sound, that makes a difference.**

**Children remember them so easily, and once they hear them, speak them while they play . . . like swinging, or jumping.**

**One good thing is how children join in with a refrain, both in poetry and stories.**

**We ought to encourage reproducing sounds. We think of it as belonging to the very young children, but it is really for all ages. It shows how well you hear.**

**I never knew children say so many rhyming chants.**

**I am going to listen more carefully when children compare things. It's language and imagination.**

60

I think just talk may be one of the most important things we do.

Children don't have much time for talking about *real* things. We forget how much they are aware of things going on in the world, like war, and strikes. They need a time to talk about these things.

Children don't have many listeners now. Parents are too busy. Maybe a teacher needs to do a lot of listening.

It would encourage children to talk more if there was always a listener.

Not talking about a *topic,* but the things that concern them, things they worry about, wonder about, or feel deeply about.

## THE DISCOVERY CENTER
"Look at everything as though you have never seen it before."

Paul Valery, philosopher

This center was a place for "found" things brought in from walks around the grounds, or surrounding neighborhood. Assorted things that were intriguing for shape and size and color. Things to feel of, look at, smell, wonder about. A pile of eucalyptus leaves with hard, pungent smelling buds, a tiny fern, a dead beetle, a rusted spring, part of a clock, a bird feather, a red button. A piece of green glass bottle to look through, a strip of blue cloth.

Ordinary things that can be found everywhere. Set them apart here and you find surprising qualities, small details of form and texture that surprise you. The almost invisible lines on the hard shell of the beetle, the tiny hairs on the stem of the fern. This is how you "stoke the imagination."

Take a clump of ordinary grass. The blades are not simply green. When you look more closely, there is orange, red, blue and a little purple. And at the base of each blade, a luminous pearl white; the dark brown earth around the roots has the smell of a damp cellar; the tiny roots are like "hair," "like weaving," "like lace" and as you turn your finger up the wrong way, the edge of the grass is rough, like a tiny saw or "a small file." Hold one blade between your thumbs, and you remember how to make a shrill tone.

And always a supply here of boxes, jars, or bags for collecting things. When you are alive to the world around you, you always find surprising things. You want to show them to others and share your feeling.

Thoughts about discovering:

**When you keep watching, you *always* find something.**

**It is unexpected, you don't know *what* will turn up.**

**We found a brick with a rough design on it and took it back to make some prints.**

**When you know there is a place for things you find, it makes you watch and collect.**

**There is no reason why a classroom can't have a discovery-table going on all the time.**

**Children like to add to it. So does the teacher.**

**I had forgotten how important nature things are . . . they lead to questions and talking.**

**You experience a sense of discovery you had almost forgotten about.**

## THE CENTER FOR LISTENING AND LOOKING

This center, at one corner of the room, was loosely walled off and could be made dark when needed to show films and slides.

It might be used by a single individual or by a group. Films available were from many different schools, in other parts of the country; slides of the play equipment and the arrangement of Pacific Oaks Children's School; a variety of short films, to encourage ideas, such as *The Daisy, Pigs, Leaf,* and *Glass.*

One of special interest was brought by Alan Leitman, to show the excitement of children discovering the possibilities of printing in the classroom.

A cassette recorder and ear phones were part of the equipment here for continuing interest and exploration into new ways.

They said:

**A listening center can easily be arranged. It doesn't need a lot of space.**

**The important thing is to have these resources at hand.**

**Now that the public libraries are offering more films and more cassettes, it should be possible to have them.**

**Children want to look at a film more than once. Often over and over.**

## SPONTANEOUS CENTERS

One, a large Tri-Wall board that one of the members brought to stand at the end of the room where it could easily be seen. A place for tacking up ideas . . . questions . . . words . . . sentences about feelings. Or pictures. Or suggestions.

It was a center for ideas as they kept occurring all through the meeting, a place that spoke to everyone because it could be seen all over and everyone could answer.

They said:

**It made you think while you were working.**

**Sometimes you don't want to *say* something, and so you *write* it, and share it that way.**

**When you find a cartoon, or a design, or a picture you like, you can share it by putting it up.**

Another, a free standing piece of Tri-Wall with strings across it, like a giant weaving frame. It stood as an invitation to everyone to add things there, and so it grew, with branches of leaves,

some long strips of colored paper, some pieces of
felt cloth, some colored tissue paper woven
loosely in the strings. It became a weaving for
everyone, combining a variety of materials. It
belonged to the whole group and it became
beautiful.

**You could easily have this in a classroom. Like
making a mural with paint, you can make a weaving with everyone adding, and enjoying the
shapes and colors and the unexpected things
that appeared.**

Then, a table full of shiny cardboard boxes, all
sizes, cast off by a Pasadena department store.
Some all black, some striped black and white,
they were a kind of continuing construction all
through the meeting. As members passed it, they
stopped to pile the boxes, then change to a different way, enjoying the black-white arrangement
each time. Moveable, three dimensional, it did not
need to be a "thing." It simply was something to
enjoy.

And, a table full of potatoes, another experience
for spontaneous arrangement of shapes. Brown,
red, tan, the lumpy shapes made interesting relationships and shadows. Good to feel in the hands,
all gradations of color, there was simply pleasure
and surprise in moving them.

Some words and thoughts:

**I liked stopping what I was working on, and going
over to move the boxes around.**

**It was like an "instant sculpture." You placed
them in different arrangements . . . the black and
the striped ones.**

**You could enjoy the shapes and you could keep
changing them. Sometimes it gave you an idea
for what you wanted to do.**

**Shiny black shapes are exciting to pile up.**

**I had never seen red potatoes before.**

**The potatoes were all colors, sort of pink, and**

purple. I discovered the shapes are really beautiful, rounded and lumpy.

I'm going to see potatoes in a new way after this.

## CENTER FOR THINKING AND BROWSING

**"never try to create and analyze at the same time. They are different processes."**
**Corita Kent, artist**

This area, arranged at one end of the room, was open yet separated by low dividers, serving as a quiet place apart from the "doing." It was a place for gestation of ideas and feelings, that part of the rhythm of the processes of imagination when ideas need to rest and deepen, when perspectives come clear. A place for thinking or talking with others or simply watching the whole room. A place for renewal of questions, of finding new directions.

*quiet place*

One part of this center was arranged with cushions and mats on the floor, flexible and welcoming, respecting those who wished to be alone, or with others. A second part of the area contained bookshelves and a round table for stopping to browse through the selection of books made available from the Pacific Oaks Library by Myrtle Stukkjaer, Librarian, and her assistants.

Books concerned with the whole span of *being.* Bronowski's *Identity of Man,* Albert Sszent-Gyorgy's *The Crazy Ape,* Loren Eiseley's *The Unexpected Universe,* and *The Feast of Fools* by Harvey Cox, and J. R. R. Tolkien's, *The Fellowship of the Ring.*

Books discussing basic values in education, with new perspectives, new insights. *The Perfect Education* by Kenneth Eble; *Education and Ecstasy* by George Leonard; *Visual Thinking* by Rudolph Arnheim; *Education and the Significance of Life* by Krishnamurti.

Books and pamphlets concerned with teaching. *The Nursery School* by Katherine Read Baker; *A Nursery School Handbook* by Green and Woods; *The Open Classroom,* Herbert Kohl; *Push Back the Desks,* Albert Cullum; *Inside the Primary School,* John Blackie; *Teaching with Feeling,*

Herbert Greenberg; *The Fives and Sixes Go To School*, Emma Sheehy.

Books about children and how they grow. *The Magic Years*, Selma Fraiberg; *Can't You Hear Me Talking to You*, Carolyn Mithes; *The Poetry of Children*, Michael Baldwin; *36 Children*, Herbert Kohl; *A House of Children*, Joyce Cary; *Dandelion Wine*, Ray Bradbury.

Books that describe the processes of imagination. *The Creative Process*, Brewster Ghiselin; *Creative Experience*, Rosner and Abt; *The Creative Process in Young Children*, Polly McVickar; *The Shape of Content*, Ben Shahn.

Books and pamphlets related to the languages of imagination. Of art: *Art for the Family*, Victor D'Amico, Museum of Modern Art, New York; *Children's Art*, Miriam Lindstrom, San Francisco Art Museum; *Child Art*, Sir Herbert Read; *Notebooks*, Paul Klee.

Of music and dance: *There's Music in Children*, Emma Sheehy; *Children Discover Music and Dance*, Emma Sheehy; *And a Time to Dance*, Norma Conner; *Music and Imagination*, Aaron Copland.

Of language: *Language, Thought and Reality*, writings of Benjamin Whorf; *Freeing Children to Write*, Mauree Applegate; *Children and Poetry*, Polly McVickar; *From Two to Five*, Kornei Chukovsky; *The Lore and Language of School-Children*, Iona and Peter Opie.

Of science: *Science and Human Values*, Bronowski; *The Immense Journey* and *Firmament of Time*, Loren Eiseley; *Development of Scientific Concepts*, John Navarra; *The Earth Beneath Us*, Kirtley Mather.

Browsing together with others, adult or child, lights up new ideas, and stirs new questions. Every age finds interest in such books of photographs as *Playtime in Africa* by Efua Theodora Sutherland, *The Family of Man* by Steiglitz, or Margaret Mead's *Family*. Photographs of paintings, drawings, constructions, suggest new ways of seeing. Browsing is a way of "looking in" on

66

other ways, of going beyond ourselves, through interest and curiosity.

In this center, too, a selection of children's books, chosen for excellent language as well as for content, written by such authors as Taro Yashima, Leo Lionni, Robert McCloskey, Eleanor Lattimore, E. B. White, Eleanor Estes. Books with fine illustrations done by artists such as Roger Duvoisin, Maurice Sendak, Barbara Cooney, Garth Williams.

Books of poetry: *Wind Song* by Carl Sandburg; *Catch Me a Wind,* Patricia Hubbell; *Take Sky* by David McCord and others by Elizabeth Coatsworth, Gwendolyn Brooks, Langston Hughes, May Swenson.

And stories of all kinds, family stories, folk tales, myths; stories of other countries, other people. Talk and thought and wonder grow into a wider awareness of life.

Spontaneously children retreat, for privacy, and for doing nothing. And then return to activity, renewed. It is a rhythm that the business of adult life seldom respects. A child once said this, firmly and strongly. As she stood before the easel doing nothing, a teacher (who wanted to see everyone busy) asked, "What are you doing?" And the child replied, "I'm wasting time." Firmly she knew her own need.

From . . .

## WHAT IS MUSIC FOR YOUNG CHILDREN
Elizabeth Jones, Pacific Oaks Faculty

In the long run, it is the teacher who remains
the crucial element in providing a curriculum of
music for children in the nursery school. In planning meaningful experiences, in recognizing and
following children's interests, in making use of
music for children's sake, good teaching remains
paramount.

a knowledge of resources in music

a comfortableness in using them (which is
perhaps most likely to stem from a feeling
that music is not something "special" for
the experts only)

recognition that what is music cannot be
pigeonholed into a few preconceived cate-
gories

sensitivity to what children are doing

willingness to learn from them

Exciting music in the nursery school does not
just happen. It reflects vital interest and knowledge manifested in good teaching.

Publication of NAEYC

Thoughts from the group:

**Teachers are always interrupting children.**

**We make them feel they ought to be busy . . . and that makes them feel they should not stop and do nothing.**

**How can thinking happen when you are always doing?**

**Perhaps children's most important growth happens when they are not outwardly doing anything.**

**We need to waste time.**

**We ought to respect rhythm, the rhythm of doing, then stopping, then going on.**

**We can judge a lot about the curriculum of the day by thinking about ourselves, and the ways we feel.**

# Insights and Learnings

**"What matters in learning is not to be taught but to wake up."**

This was a meeting for *waking up.*

Out of experiencing came renewed insights and enlarged understandings of the universal processes of imagination. For each, there seemed three aspects. First, as *self* giving value to the inner unpredictable directions of imagination in every part of life; second, as *teacher* concerned for carrying out the wholeness of learning experience with students and children; and third, simply as *humanist* concerned for deeper understanding of others, especially the vital and strong thrust of children in life experiences.

## AS SELF

Although it had many forms, the fundamental process was similar for all. The *taking-in process,* not only awareness of the immediate environment, but the continual drawing on the individual storehouse of sensory remembrance, knowledge, experience, feeling, understanding. And out of that, the *making,* perhaps an abstract idea, a thing with form and shape and color, or a song or dance. Here we saw evidence of the continuing circle of human function, taking in and giving out, speaking through the languages of the imagination.

These are some of the words:

I felt that all the creative ideas I had had for years had been pushed aside, but in this environment, with others, all working together, that storehouse of thought and imagination came to life.

The taking-in process was different for everyone. Some looked around the whole room slowly, others looked quickly and began to work.

You felt it was important to look at everything.

It helped you to feel free about where you wanted to begin, what materials you wanted to use.

We tend to hurry over the taking-in process, and we hurry children over it.

74

It was important to take your time, you could not hurry it.

About the room, you could watch the whole of it as you worked, because the dividers were low and it was all open.

The taking-in process went on all the time. You kept getting suggestions from what you saw and what others were doing.

You found things you hadn't noticed before.

It was important to take time for seeing, feeling, smelling, the sensory things at each center. You became aware of details you hadn't noticed before. You had time to take your time.

Because the materials were grouped in each center, it made a loose kind of order.

You saw where things were and when you wanted a material or a tool, you knew where to get it, right then, without hunting around.

Sometimes you found things you didn't know were there.

The basic order helped direct your mind to what you wanted to do.

You could see what to select, or reject, or try out.

In the evening, when I wasn't there, I found myself thinking about what I would do when I returned. I thought of the things that were there.

It was like planning ahead. You began making what you wanted, in your mind. Then you did it the next day.

Really, you keep taking things in all your life, and when you come to work with clay, or paint, or wood, all your sensory remembrance, your experiences in the past come to the fore. Not just the taking in right now.

You draw on all of yourself, your whole storehouse of logic and memory, intelligence, feelings, intuitions, humor.

The process of making begins when an idea, or combination of ideas and feeling is so insistent and meaningful, it must find some language of expression—dance, or music, or art or language, or science concept.

The selection of a starting point, in movement or tone or color or words is made by the individual. It is his individual choice. And the starting point is only a beginning place, for there may be any combination of media as the idea tells you. But with each step, you the individual make that choice. What next? What if? Add this. Change that, another color, another material. You work until what you make fits the idea.

It is a circular process and that is its significance. Your idea tells your hands; and your hands explore and learn, and tell your mind the next direction. It is total growth.

**I never knew all the materials could belong together.**

**I had thought of art as paint, and carpentry as construction, both separate. Here everything was combined—wood, paper, paint, sawdust, cloth, leaves, clay, grasses.**

**You could move from one center to another as you worked out an idea.**

**It could be a thing, or expression of a feeling.**

**There was no right or wrong, no good or bad. Rightness was when the materials used exactly expressed the idea. You were the judge of that.**

Making had many directions, many forms. It might be something wholly *new* and uniquely the product of individual imagination.

**My clay shape was, for me, pleasing and interesting, and I wanted to keep it that way.**

**I found a piece of wood that reminded me of a rocker, and by adding paint and cloth to it, I made a thing that brought a whole experience into existence.**

76

A painting is more like a map of your route.

When you set out to make a "picture" you constrict yourself. You are not open to all the suggestions that come from the material.

It might be the *rearrangement* of some given shapes or forms.

The set of boxes could be glued together in any pattern I wished.

Bells in the music center were rearranged in space and sequence to make different tones and reverberations.

Wood shapes tied together made wooden chimes, that, played with a record, became a spontaneous dance.

From . . .

## WHAT CHILDREN TELL US

**Frank Sata, Architect**
**Pacific Oaks faculty**

Every adult has the potential of providing a posi-
tive experience for the child. A space enriched to
motivate response is dependent on the sensitivity
of the adult to recognize growth and change.
When the excitement of discovery and exploration diminishes, it is possible to again initiate
some type of change on the environment. This
could be as simple as changing displays, shifting
furniture, or creating projects to be displayed.
Sun and plant life are vital to the child, and we
must make an effort to preserve the language of
nature as an element of his culture. An artificial
environment can only enhance an artificial
culture.

Movement in space is structured by the place-
ment of objects in that space. A static space is
one which can be symmetrical and structured to
straight line movements . . . an organic space
might require more dexterity and ingenuity for the
individual. . . . It is usually a space in constant
change, for the child is constantly changing and
growing. . . .

It might be changing something by *adding* another element.

**Some wood scraps already with a pattern suggested paint and glue in the depression areas to show a whole new design.**

**A long piece of hung cloth suggested places where paper and streamers were added.**

It might be *inventing* something for a purpose.

**In the woodworking center, I found I could make holes in tubing and have a pipe to blow.**

**With a pattern and suggestions, Tri-Wall became a book rack.**

**Winding string around the Tri-Wall piece . . . of wood, I made a loom.**

Or a *fantasy* idea, a thing that has never been.

**A clay place developed, in imaginary parts, a sort of castle with a moat and leaves added to be trees.**

**I made a curious animal of clay with leaf ears, stick tail. Like an animal but not like one that is known, really.**

Sometimes it is important to *destroy*.

**When you have worked a long time and can't seem to make it be what you want, it gives your ideas a fresh start.**

**The decision to destroy may be a really creative act.**

**Sometimes it makes you feel good to destroy something and start again.**

Making means work, hard work, because the individual is himself his own stern critic.

You learn as you work. Your idea drives you forward.

I learned about tools and what they can do.

A small brush does one kind of thing, a broad one speaks in a different way.

I kept learning as I went along.

You learn the most from things that don't work. Then you find the thing that will.

The materials make suggestions, and what your muscles do suggest the next step and the next.

You have to be open to what turns up.

It matters that the tools are good, and are kept that way. Good brushes, good saws, well mixed clay.

What does *"finish"* mean?

Sometimes you work too hard to finish what you are doing. You push at it and then it isn't how you want it.

It is better to put something aside when you feel hurried to "finish."

You need to wait, maybe think about something else.

Work on it the next day when you are fresh.

By waiting, you get some new ideas.

We should never hurry children to finish. It doesn't happen that way.

Sometimes you see how you can change the idea and make it better.

You learn a lot when you are making something. You learn about the materials and mostly you learn about yourself.

From . . .

**IMAGINATION AND OUTDOOR PLAY**
**Elizabeth Prescott**

The way in which play space is organized and the kind of things you put in it, determine to a great extent what kinds of imaginative choices will happen.

Swings with fixed seats make one kind of experience, but if the seats can be changed and adjusted to different heights it makes possible a whole range of exploration. The arc of a high swing is much different in rhythm and feeling and can lead to a variety of ideas.

In the Pacific Oaks Yards, the cargo nets are hung by the four corners and by this arrangement, encourage highly diverse activity. They invite group play that frequently leads to chanting and singing in time with the rhythm as children exert whole body motions to make the nets move. Or they become a place for imaginative play—"We are in a spider web."

Use of space provides a good way to think of what you are doing, why you are doing it, and what the possibilities may be.

Very early in the meeting, awareness of two processes came clear. Indeed, that two kinds of meaning would happen. *First,* the total experience of discovery and exploration of trying out ideas and feelings through making and doing, each person experiencing his own affirmation through the languages of imagination. *Second,* the full import of the meeting would not come until after the experience when the routes and the processes of imagination could be seen more clearly, and out of that, the specific learnings and insights for teaching.

Certainly, along with the work and experiencing, there were many conversations going on, exchange of questions, wondering, suggestions. Talk concerning materials, and ways of using them, or combining in different ways. Mainly discussion of individual directions as imagination developed and extended.

Out of the experiencing, each would go away with his own individual insights. Experience and imagination is a private process, but it is also universal and the fact that talk and discussion flowed so easily demonstrated this.

Out of experiencing, each would return to his own life setting and would draw new awareness and understandings which would, with certainty, apply in the experience of teaching others.

But the meanings would take time to be absorbed and the implications would not appear all at once. Some aspects might not come clear until they were tried out in school experience.

Two questions were sent to each participant, asking whether the experiences had been of meaning in a personal context, and if they had used and developed some new and imaginative directions.

As the responses showed, the space of elapsed time gave a chance for perspective and for trying out new ways. Thought and remembrance and feelings had time to surface.

New understanding of what "freedom" means.

**It has helped me to see the processes of imagination and to know this is what matters.**

Sometimes the process takes a long time, at other times very short.

I am not as free as I want to be yet, but I am moving and I can be flexible and can help the processes of imagination as I see it happen with children.

I am allowing my children more freedom in all creative areas and consequently I am more free and relaxed. Every day is more enjoyable.

In being more free, I have time to observe individual needs and have the opportunity to meet them.

Time has new relevance. Large blocks of time have been made larger, and teachers have become more free to work with individuals or small groups.

I have a new look at freedom and what we mean by it.

New directions in basic thinking.

Interest centers have been expanded to be more available to *all* children in *all* of our classes.

Now I understand how children must feel when the teacher suddenly wants them to stop. When I was working with the materials, I did not want to be interrupted. Now I let children continue as long as possible.

I found new media and new ways of expression.

We have assessed our activities to make them more open, more child-oriented and more creative.

I learned how to plan and provide experience for children and then stand back, ready to encourage and support.

I learned how to plan and provide experiences for children and we find mutual pleasure in it. I often learn from them some new way that I had not thought of. We work together.

From . . .

**WHAT NOW?**
**Dr. Alan Leitman**
**Education Development Center**
**Newton, Massachusetts**

Dr. Leitman proposed the idea that very few
people would be able to carry out the experiences of this meeting.

The group answered him:

**I have found new feelings and new ideas.**

**There is no material and no idea here that I can-
not use in some way with my teachers and
parents, and with the children of my school.**

**By letting ideas take shape, in wood and paint
and clay, I have found out that "making" is the
most important thing we can do, at any age.
Children and teachers.**

**Now we have found out what to aim for. It gives
us direction and new values.**

**If the experience here has meant something in
our own lives, if it has awakened our capacity to
imagine, then it is of deep and lasting value.**

**Imagination in Action**

In specific areas of school planning:

I found a much more relaxed approach to teaching *science.* Science is not a final fact. It changes all the time. What a child finds out for himself is right, it is his own. I learned to let him find it himself, even though I see it may be incorrect.

We have changed our *playground* area as a result of ideas we found in the Pacific Oaks playground.

We discovered the way to hang cargo nets . . . by the four corners.

I saw the importance of a wide range of *books* for children.

I realized that *browsing,* looking through books is as important as hearing them read aloud.

A separate place for books, apart from activity is important. They should always be there.

I took a great deal back to Alaska, especially a new understanding of *movement* and *creative dance.*

I am using *music* in a much more relaxed way. I see it is a natural way of expression, and a natural way of enjoyment.

New directions in art

*Art* **is not just for school, it is something to do any time and in any place. We need to help children know that. I am planning for much more diversity.**

**In art, especially, the choices are important.**

**I got a whole new feeling for clay and what it means to an adult, or a child.**

**I found the excitement of knowing how to use woodworking tools and materials.**

**This is what Piaget is saying about learning . . . "they must be able to try things out to see what happens, manipulate objects, pose questions . . . and seek answers."**

**My own ideas of learning through self-discovery were reinforced in this rich environment.**

**Now I know how children feel.**

**I see children in myself.**

With parent groups

**I took back to my group of thirty poverty parents, many subtle feelings that came to me in this meeting. I could see how the ease and openness of this meeting might be planned in their groups.**

**Our parent meetings were enriched and we are planning a similar kind of workshop so that parents can discover and explore, and better understand the common interests they share with their children.**

With teachers and students new understanding of freedom and new recognition that "why we do what we do," gives a base for what is taught.

**I have taken back a more relaxed approach in working with teachers on curriculum—what we are doing, why, and how being aware of imaginative processes, we are reaching goals that are important for all children.**

I found new ways to keep imagination alive, in all areas of the day.

We have reorganized a class for teachers with the basic approach of the conference.

In staff meetings, we have enriched our plans not only in what actually takes place, but in feeling the need for creative effort in all human life.

We have coordinated an Art Workshop at our college.

We wanted to make this approach known to the community and arranged an open meeting where everyone could explore and discover and imagine.

The most important question is "what if." No area of teaching is closed.

When you let yourself become imaginative in one area of interest, it stirs up *all* areas.

You catch the spirit of exploring and letting yourself use your imagination when you are with others who are also extending imagery and ideas.

From this meeting, I pulled myself out of my rut, and new ideas and creative thoughts came faster than I could believe.

We can probably say of teaching itself, that when the question "what if" is allowed to enter and function, then it follows that the teacher and the environment become alive, open to new ideas, open to experiments and trying new ways. And learning itself becomes alive for children.

Kenneth Eble has said it well, in *The Perfect Education,*

If I were to ask one thing above all others of teachers, it would be imagination . . . the kind of mind that is playful, fanciful, odd in the relationships it perceives, that actively connects things as they are with things as they might be, that always pokes into corners and comes up with that which excites laughter or wonder.

## AS HUMANIST
**"Now I know how children feel."**

As the meeting developed and each teacher became involved with doing and making and feeling, this was heard again and again. The spontaneous connection between our own experiencing and what we know of children's experiences.

It is impossible to ever create a wholly ideal environment, and indeed it would probably bring us to a standstill. But we can establish the most feasible environment possible in terms of what we value, in terms of available resources, time and space, and materials and tools. When the aim is clear, and we are moving toward that, then alternatives suggest themselves.

It takes some imaginative planning, some looking ahead. Making time and space for the processes of imagination to happen in the experience of children is much more a question of attitude than the actual form of the environment.

About time

**I think even very young children have this sense about their making, that they want to "finish it" when their idea tells them it is completed.**

**We can give them an attitude about time. The awareness that just because the minutes have ended, it does not mean that the idea and the "making" have ended.**

**We convey a sense of "on-going" time, by putting work aside to return to at a later time.**

**The sense of "on-going" means a safe and protected place for it to be kept. "Made things" are visible evidence of ideas and feelings, and represent strong affirmation of self. They should be regarded as such.**

**The fact of a place for keeping is, in itself, evidence of respect for ideas and making. Respect for your own making and respect for the making of others.**

**It represents a way of thinking and a way of working; that an idea is important.**

## About space

It is probable no school can ever have the amount of space that is wholly adequate; but like time, an attitude about space is what matters.

**You have to invent space when children have something going. You "make do" using every inch there is . . . the floor, table tops, under tables, shelf areas, putting boards across chairs.**

**The important thing is the idea. Some ideas take a small space, others need a large area; so you adapt and adjust.**

**Children understand this. It too is a kind of respect for work. When one child is needing much space, then it is easily understood that others give way. It is all part of a cooperative for needs. They know that when *they* need enlarged space, others will make it possible.**

**When you *feel* this out of your own experience, as we have here, then you *know* how it can be for children.**

**Space is flexible and when an unfinished project stands in the middle of the room until finished, the inconvenience of crowding is not an inconvenience. It's making the space work, and making an idea happen.**

## About materials and tools

**It matters a lot that the tools are in good condition; saws that are sharp, scissors oiled at the point of moving, glue that flows, paint that is rich in color, clay the consistency that is workable.**

**It is discouraging, and cuts off ideas, if you have to stop to soften clay.**

**It makes you "mad" when a tool or a material you want is not there. It cuts off the idea when you have to hunt and search.**

**Some basic order is important in clarifying your idea and clarifying the making. The tools that you see, make a suggestion to you; and your idea tells you the tool you want. It works both ways.**

Part of the making process, is taking care of tools. Cleaning brushes and glue dispensers, means that it is ready for the next person . . . and perhaps that next one is you.

Materials suggest ways of working.

# Imagination as Life Experience

**"Push back the desks."**
**Albert Cullum**

## SCHOOLS—Guardians of Human Potential

New ways and new directions in education are beginning to appear, but only beginning. Open education is letting the imaginative processes in the door.

Alternative elementary schools are challenging children to raise questions and make their own discoveries. Fresh, new, based in their own perceptions and logic. Not of a book, not finding what the books say will be there, but finding uniquely what is there in terms of a child's own knowing.

The Parkway Project in Philadelphia showed us a new kind of high school, relevant learning that is alive because it is life experience.

At the college level, Pacific Oaks is extending some new directions and raising new questions and arriving at new possibilities for study that respects individual pursuits and interests. In the preparation of teachers, we believe that when students experience the routes of imagination, they are then able to encourage and value the imaginative thrust of children in the classroom.

Dr. E. Robert LaCrosse, President of Pacific Oaks, has written, "We are a school of process." Changing, growing, challenging established ideas, letting new ones in, making some mistakes and learning from those, these are part of the processes of imagination.

We are committed to showing, by our own way of education, the belief we hold for imaginative experiences in the classrooms where our students go to teach.

We say that a school must not be remote from life experience, but must indeed *be* life experience.

Not a place where it is "wrong" to ask questions; not "wrong" to suggest and try out new and unknown ways; not "wrong" to make a mistake and not failure when you don't "get it right."

Rather we are talking about an environment where the teacher is human and honest, and where it is a sign of learning to ask questions and raise preposterous ideas. A place where you try things out to see if they will work and where the teacher herself is learning and experiencing.

An environment in which the relationship of teachers and children is one of joy and excitement in exploring and knowing. Where teachers trust children and where children trust each other and respect the different ways of all. A place where there are the sounds of talk and laughter and music and work going on and where everyday new and unexpected discoveries are made.

Especially an environment where there are choices of materials and where imagination has a chance to work with more than one or two possibilities, where the process of learning *how* to select and reject, or weigh values and possibilities, means the growth of judgment and knowledge; where there is a chance to try out what everyone says will *not* work; but there is value for the need to find that out for yourself; and the opportunity to use tools and materials, and work at an idea to make it happen.

An environment where the human relationships of feelings and thoughts interweave and work together and where there can be openness of talk and discussion when something is not working well, just as it happens at every level, child or adult.

Adapted from . . .

**THE COOPERATIVE NURSERY SCHOOL:**
Educational Responsibility
Polly McVickar, Pacific Oaks faculty

Fundamental to the whole is a belief in people
and a belief in ideas. When the procedures of the
children's school or the adult group seem out of
balance, the group asks itself one question,
"What can we do about it?"

The answer comes out of a continuing thought
for the whole and its parts, taking a renewed look
at the plan in terms of its values, or changing
arrangements and action.

This is the dynamic and creative quality of the
cooperative nursery schools. They are never
static. Change and growth take place as feelings
and ideas and educational directions come
together. There is always more than one way of
doing. *"What if?" "What else?"*

Both the growth of the group and of the individual
has its own pace. It never takes place evenly, not
all at the same time. There will be stops and
starts; times when things move fast and times
when nothing seems to go. The recognition of
the process is important in understandings and
action.

The director herself must be able to say, "I just
don't know," and then, with the group, move in a
direction drawn out of knowledge and experience and judgment.

The underlying belief, "we can" establishes a
sense of openness and flexibility and leads to
new, fresh, imaginative ideas.

Publication of NAEYC

## IMAGINATION—HUMAN CENTER

This meeting was a demonstration of process—
active, changing, growing—over the three-day
period. From engagement of self-directed begin-
nings in all areas of interest, it became an experience both individual and group. Each person
worked toward results that were wholly unpredictable, yet definite in the learnings that emerged.
And to the extent that everyone explored and
learned, the shared learnings became suggestions
and insights for everyone. It was total experience
and total learning.

The central processes of imagination were free
and relatively uninterrupted. New thought and new
ways came about as a renewed belief in the
human imagination began to grow. Ideas out of
the past, imagining the future, enlarging the present, the experience was a reaffirmation of self,
and reinforcement of individual power to make
something new, to change what exists, and to
never cease challenging and questioning.

Time, space, materials, tools. This is the frame-
work with which we are dealing, whether we are
concerned with actual materials or abstract ideas.
Most often they are not separate, for the meanings
of one interweave with the other.

In **"exercising the muscles of the imagination,"**
the ingredients of the processes came clear.
Doing is not simply "making." It is much more.
In the making and exploring, insights emerge that
cannot come by talk and discussion. Both are
significant and each extends the other. Both are
cognitive as the process of discernment, selection, rejection, choice, trial and error make
learning.

Susan Cohen, one of the student teachers at
Pacific Oaks, has written about the relationship of
teacher and student and learning, and because
her words extend and amplify what this meeting
found, they make clear how imagination is the
key to the unexpected capacities of life, the
human potential.

100

1. Imagination as the nucleus from which the individual moves out in all directions:

**Clay is a beautiful thing in itself, to touch and move. I found ways of moving the clay . . . freely in my hands, and carefully, forcefully centering it and myself. My hands were my tools. I found ways that seemed to be inside of me already and I was somehow just discovering a part of me. Through curiosity comes imagining.**

**Suddenly everything relates to the clay . . . the color of a tree's bark, of its leaves, of the earth itself . . . the texture of a sidewalk, of a piece of glass, the smell of wet earth . . . all are part of my interest and my use of clay. What would happen if . . . I begin to combine things differently in my head.**

Here was the importance of letting a fresh material unfold. The physical motion of hands, the doing, gives idea and feeling to the mind; and from that the mind gives ideas and direction to the hands.

Sensory knowing is part of it, and relating like-nesses. It is taking time to know clay in how it feels and smells, how the shapes look, how the shadows come, how the color changes as it dries. The individual thinks and grows as sensory exploration moves.

2. Imagination as a means of freeing the individual to try out experiences, feelings, ideas, that go beyond conformity:

**Once you begin it's a matter of trying something and watching what happens. Ah, you can say, that didn't work, but then this might. You rediscover in the work of others around you, possibilities that have been explored and combined, what has worked for them . . . and you hold onto that discovery slowly making it your own and in a new way seeing a way of combining, of creating. And then it is yours and you take a new step beyond.**

Sometimes combining ideas in your head, or feeling how another feeling would be. When you make with your hands, it is what Miriam Lindstrom says, **"You take out of yourself a feeling or an idea and** place it where you can see it, and sense it, and extend it further. You try out things that come to you out of past experiences, out of present knowing, and you make new relationships that have not been made before."

When you make, or invent, or change something, you are in a way, talking with yourself. You are trying out, you are rephrasing life and asking the question, "what if . . . ."

3. Imagination as the root of cognitive activity through discovering, exploring, knowing:

What you find out by exploring, extends the language of your imagination. Your skill grows, and new ways appear. The idea you have is what will direct the form of what you make. Not what someone tells you, not what a book says, though it may give you important suggestions, but the form of the thing is right only when it accords with the idea in your head. Then there is a sense of being finished.

Each time you explore the properties of clay and the way it works, the more you are acquainted with it, the closer it comes to becoming what you want. Your skill increases.

You try new tools, you make your own tools, and the end will be a surprise because you have used your intelligence and your feelings and your questions: you have let it grow and change. There is a sense of knowing, of new familiarities, that says you are learning.

4. Imagination as it is enhanced or stifled by attitudes in the educational environment:

If we feel free to listen and to watch each other, we can discover ourselves more naturally. My greatest teachers have been those who are students with me. Being able to watch how another explores the same idea, the same materials, the same feeling, enhances my own imagining.

To be given a separate piece of paper, in a separate corner, where I am "to know" (not discover) answers, (which is not knowledge) to certain

102

**unrelated questions, has most stifled my imagination. Learning to relate ourselves to the happenings of ourselves and others is the most important freedom there is. You can trust yourself. And teachers should have that sense of trust in students, at every age.**

We began with people and the capacity to imagine. Specifically we began with ourselves. We established a base of sensory awareness and out of that the *starting points* for the arts and sciences. These are the languages by which human beings speak and how our ideas come about in art, music, dance, language, movement, science and the whole realm of social relationships.

When the human imagination draws on *past* remembrances and experiences, or thinks ahead to what might be in the *future*, or enlarges the *present* through insight and doing and trying— then the wholeness of an idea and the wholeness of the person happens.

Sir Herbert Read says, "The foundation of a civilization rests not in the mind but in the senses." This is where we all have a starting point. This meeting demonstrated how, when the centers were ready as starting points, growth and learning took place—and do so in the classroom.

# Sources of Quotes